A Musician's DICTIONARY

SOUND AND VISION

A Musician's DICTIONARY

David W. Barber

CARTOONS
Dave Donald

SOUND AND VISION

AUTHOR'S NOTE
AND ACKNOWLEDGEMENTS

As work progressed on this book and before I had decided upon its title, I grew tired of having constantly to refer to it as "my book" or "the book I'm working on." And so it came to be known simply as SAM — which doesn't stand for anything. It was just that I already had a book named FRED in the works, and SAM was more polite than "hey you." And so it is as SAM that I still know it. It still usually answers to that name.

There are many people who — by way of advice, encouragement or otherwise — were helpful at various stages in the production of this book. To them I offer my warmest acknowledgements and thanks. Chief among these are the members of my family and my friends for their support and encouragement. And thanks to Geoff Savage of Sound And Vision and to Dave Donald for their help in this revised and expanded edition.

DWB
Westport and Toronto, 1997

PREFACE

Those wedded to music belong to the realm of the constant-ephemeral — a visionary realm requiring oft-time the painful renunciation of reality — remember those glorious images of spirit rendered flesh — of divinity — of beauty of princes and princesses condemned to a yearning for even the shortest-lived mortal incarnation — and oft-times lending that alternative dimension, introspective or objective, as the case may be, to one's own life.

A musician's humor is the inevitable distillation of a capacity to listen to himself, honestly to take blame for his own mistakes and shortcomings, a freedom from prejudice and an ability to see himself in as unreal and ludicrous a light as others might see him, this extra-terrestrial being — messenger, clown, seer, priest or demon — exposing and liberating us to ourselves in the deepest sense possible and without the accusatory embarrassment of words. For humor is the gift of the gods — born of deep humanity, of suffering and compassion, as of that divine and somewhat remote disattachment it promotes the same creative originality of observation which reveals the mysteries of Nature to the born scientist as the mysteries of human nature to the born artist.

Musicians are, generally, irrepressible in their exuberance, passion and curiosity. Usually, if they are real musicians, they are, as such, essential and irresistible to their mortal fellow-women and fellow-men. They form a curious breed blessed with the eye and ear of the beholder, thus able to make fun of themselves and perhaps, more through humor than philosophy, cheat, if only fleetingly, the very powers of darkness and tragedy which stalk the path of life.

This amusing and witty book has only one omission, i.e. the pianist, who, as a genuinely profound musician taking my teasing in good grace, must be a magician. Having a brilliant pianist as my son (Jeremy by name) my imagination has been exhaustively exercised in commenting — of course disparagingly (for that is the very essence of humor) — on this out-of-tune piece of furniture, which can serve in so many other capacities than music — for instance a bar or nice flat surface to stretch out on, as the case may be. Shark-like it displays a menacing lower denture of black and white teeth; a more rational disposition of this lower denture in the proper half-circle has been tried but abandoned, no doubt owing to the increased difficulty of turning pages — also called keyboard, to which the pianist, countering with an upper denture of ill-fitting and bleeding fingers, hammers and grinds out (with the help of additional hammers hidden in the bowels of the beast) a percussive noise of simultaneous notes, called harmony — obviously so dubbed because these notes are in fact short-lived, falsely pitched, aggressive. Therefore the great pianist is, as I tell my son Jeremy, a good magician, for by sheer will and imagination he conveys the ecstasy of music through means which are therefore a compromise. The keyboard has never developed into a proper typewriter, for the alphabet is unmarked and in no case extends beyond the letter G, and it is further devoid of numerals. For these reasons pianists do not make successful secretaries. I am in no doubt that the publisher is reserving an entire book on this vast subject.

And now, having attempted to throw a spadeful of grit into this delightful book, may I offer my best wishes to the reader, who will share and perchance enjoy a sample of musician's humor — from one of this laugh-able stock.

Yehudi Menuhin

DEDICATION

For Brian Law, who first taught me
that music can laugh, with all due respect.

Le monde est plein de fous,
et qui n'en veut pas voir,
doit se tenir tout seul,
et casser son miroir.

Thomas Love Peacock
(*Crotchet Castle*, 1831)

And for Judy, for everything she has done over the
years to help, support and encourage me.

Per ardua ad Astrid

Audience Participation

A

Accidentals: Wrong notes.

Acoustics: The science of sound, and the study of how music misbehaves in various physical environments. Most useful as a scapegoat to explain why the performer(s) sound bad — "How can anyone perform in a space like this?" and so on.

Action: In a piano, the term used to describe the behavior of the mechanism that produces the sound. The action may be considered "light," "heavy," "stiff" and so on. Also, the term a pianist might use to describe activities that are more recreational in nature. This sort of action might be considered "slow," "hot," "lucky" and so on.

Air: 1. A simple tune, often for a singer.
2. What the singer must have before performing such a tune.
3. In the plural (airs), what the singer puts on after performing such a tune particularly well.

Aleatoric Music: Any form of music composition (but especially in modern music) that relies on elements of chance for its production — such as provided by the tossing of coins, throwing of dice, or disbursement of artistic grants.

Altered Chord: Any chord (also called a *chromatic chord*) that contains notes other than those found in the diatonic scale of the appropriate key. In other words, a chord with wrong notes in it. Occurs frequently in jazz music, modern music and any music involving amateurs and/or small children.

Alto: (see *Contralto*).

Amen: The final word of hymns, psalms and many other religious pieces of music (originally from the Hebrew term meaning "so be it" or "you don't say?"). The musical and liturgical equivalent of saying "Enough already. Let's just go home."

Anacrusis: An unstressed note at the beginning of a musical phrase. Also called a *pickup note*. Not to be confused with *anacrisis*, a term that might apply when a performer misses the entry on such a pickup note.

Analysis: 1. A fruitless attempt at musical dissection, similar to autopsy — the result in both cases being a lifeless, dismembered corpse. The practice of music analysis is based on George Bernard Shaw's precept that "He who can, does. He who cannot, teaches."
2. What's required by many musicians, especially those who've studied music analysis.

Answer: The second melody in a fugue — which seems to imply that the first ought to be considered a question.

Anticipation: The sounding of one note before that of the others. A highbrow and more polite term for *wrong entry* or *coming in too soon*. Also, the feeling a musician gets while waiting for money to arrive in the mail. (Not to be confused with *disappointment*, the feeling the musician gets when the amount is smaller than anticipated.)

Applause: Noise made by the audience (often at the wrong time, such as in the middle of a symphony, between movements). Intended to signify congratulations, it's used almost as often to destroy the mood of a quiet piece of music, and to express a desire to end the performance and go home.

Aria: What you get when you multiply a singer's length by his or her width.

Artistic Grants: Huge sums of money given at the drop of a hat for useless musical endeavors. They are always given to *other* musicians.

Arts Council: The living embodiment of Murphy's Law ("If something can go wrong, it will") and the paramount example of Man's inhumanity to Man.

ASCAP: An association (the American Society of Composers, Authors and Publishers) founded in 1914 to represent the rights of its members. Not to be confused with *dunce cap*, an article many of them probably ought to be wearing.

Atonality: A pathological disease that affects many composers of modern music. Its most noticeable symptom is the inability to make decisions — such as what key we should be in. It's the advanced and sometimes fatal stage of *polytonality*.

Audience: A group consisting of individuals who, when afflicted by a cold, don't go to a doctor. They go instead to the concert hall, where they hack and wheeze to their heart's content. Audiences can be divided into two categories: Those who sleep with their mouths open, and those who sleep with their mouths closed.

B

Bagpipes: A Scottish instrument (of torture, war, mass destruction) whose sound resembles that of a cat being run over by a car. This poses an interesting chronological paradox, since the bagpipes were invented long before the arrival of the automobile. Historians with nothing better to do might consider this a useful thesis topic.

Band: Any group of instrumentalists, but especially those playing rock music or military tunes. Not to be confused with *banned* — which is what we might wish such groups would be.

Bar: 1. The basic measurement of music, dividing it into sections of an approximately equal number of beats, based on the reasonable assumption that musicians can't count higher than four.
2. A place of camaraderie and alcoholic consumption often frequented by musicians (and singers) before, during and after a performance.

Baritone: The male voice that lies between the bass and tenor (not unlike a shortstop in baseball), combining the negative qualities of both. Baritones have a tendency to sing a different piece of music from everyone else, and to sound like a trombone filled with cold coffee. The term is possibly derived from the Latin *boro*, which means "dunce." Most of those who think they are tenors are actually baritones, just as most baritones are really basses.

Baroque: 1. A period of music so called because the study of it leads to impoverishment.
2. A slang term of encouragement used by musicians. Best exemplified by the phrase "Go for Baroque."

Bass: The lowest vocal line, sung by men, usually old and doddering, often also blind and deaf. Basses have a tendency to sing flat, or not at all, and to sound like a pregnant foghorn. Derived from the Latin *bassus*, which means "base" (but whether in the sense of "pedestal" or "debauched" isn't entirely clear).

Bassoon: A low-pitched wind instrument, a relative of the baboon, the buffoon and the bazooka. Also easily converted into a periscope. The Italian term for bassoon is *fagotto* — which doesn't mean what you think it does.

Baton: The thin white stick used by conductors to establish the beat. Thought to have been derived from some sort of ancient fertility symbol, it's now used chiefly out of longstanding tradition. In fact, it's almost utterly useless, since nobody can actually see it. It is useful, however, for threatening recalcitrant musicians or singers, and ought to be sharpened regularly. Derived from the Latin *bastum*, from which we also get the word "bastard."

Beat: 1. The basic unit of measurement in music. It varies from piece to piece, from performance to performance, and from person to person. Using a complicated algebraic formula — based on sum totals, averages and

A Baroque Composer

A Bass

phases of the moon — the beat is established by the conductor, and then promptly ignored by all.

2. What a performer is after a performance.

Bebung: A rapid trill or vibrato (from the German for "trembling") on a string instrument or sometimes a clavichord. Beethoven and Chopin called for *bebung* in some of their piano pieces, but they were dreaming. You can't do it on a piano. Not to be confused with *bebop*, a style of music in which any trembling more likely comes from alcohol or drug abuse.

Bent: A term used to describe the shape of most valved brass instruments — trumpets, tuba, trombone and so on. By extension, then, the term is often applied to anyone who plays such an instrument (see *Heel, Nut*).

Brain: A large human organ that controls thought and reason. Distinguishes Man from lower animals and musicians from the rest of Mankind. In accordance with the principles of the theory of natural selection and evolution, the cranial space normally reserved for the brain is, in musicians, given over to lung capacity (so that they have, quite literally, blown their brains out). In singers, the absence of brain matter leaves extra room for resonance. Science has been unable to discover whether conductors have been provided with any sort of replacement for the missing brain — but that's highly unlikely.

Brass: 1. A family of orchestral instruments that includes trumpets, trombones, French horns and antique bedsteads. The development of brass instruments can be traced back to early 12th-century cisterns. Sound is produced by means of blowing or buzzing (the so-called "raspberry" or "Bronx cheer") into one end of a long, curved tube, in the hopes that the sound that comes out the other end will be less rude. In between may be any number of valves, crooks, spigots, etc. In essence, brass instruments are nothing more than elaborate spittoons. 2. Richard Strauss had this piece of advice for would-be conductors: "Never, under any circumstances, *never* look at the brass."

Break: A term with a variety of musical meanings:
1. The point in a singer's voice between the low and high registers.
2. A similar point in the register of many instruments, especially woodwinds.
3. In jazz music, the name for a middle section where a player might perform a solo.
4. In all forms of music, the name for the short rest during rehearsal, strictly enforced by union regulations.
5. In all forms of music, what you might wish to do to an instrument being performed badly — or to the person doing to performing.

Bridge: 1. The middle section of a piece of music that links the opening statement to its return in the recapitulation.
2. A small, arched piece of wood in the violin and other instruments that supports the strings.
3. A game of cards usually more enjoyable than the music of the violin or other string instruments — and an especially useful pastime if the middle section of a piece of music goes on far too long.

Bright: With many singers, especially sopranos or

tenors, a term that may be used to describe their sound quality — though rarely their intelligence.

Byrd: An important figure in the history of early English music (William Byrd, 1543-1623). So important, in fact, that many people consider early English music to be strictly "for the byrds."

C

Cadence: A device for stopping a piece of music, the musical equivalent of a brick wall. Some cadences are less complete than others, and may be called "deceptive" or "unfair" cadences. The most common form of cadence is the one called "V-I." In order to understand this, it's necessary to understand the terms "V" and "I." Sorry, can't help you.

Carol: The name of a woman we knew once who — oh, never mind.

Cello: A member of the string family, larger than both the violin and the viola. The cello is the instrument said to resemble the human voice most closely. However, it has been unable so far to grasp even the most basic principles of grammar and syntax. This is unfortunate, since its incapacity for witty conversation precludes what might otherwise have been an enjoyable lifestyle spent at dinner parties and on the talkshow circuit.

Choir: A musical organization thought to have been invented by G.F. Handel to ensure the perpetuation of performances of *Messiah*.

Church: 1. That institution largely responsible for the existence of choirs, choirmasters, organs and organists. It's also to blame for sermons, offertories and other forms of punishment.

2. The large, damp, drafty edifice that houses any or all of the above.

Coda: A short section of music tacked on to the end of a piece. The musical equivalent of "P.S."

Coloratura Soprano: A soprano with hiccups.

Comodo: A tempo indication (from the Italian meaning "leisurely" or "without strain"). Not to be confused with *commode*, a small chair containing a chamberpot — the use of which may also be leisurely (and, one hopes, without strain).

Compass: 1. Another term for range — that is, all the notes, from the lowest to highest, than an instrument is capable of playing, or a singer singing. Doesn't include screeches or squawks.

2. A device used by campers, to avoid becoming lost. Unfortunately not applicable to musicians, except while on tour.

Composer: The individual, preferably now dead (the longer the better, up to a point), who was responsible for writing the music. All of the composer's wishes regarding notes, tempo, expression and so are carefully taken down in the score, and then ignored.

Concert Hall: A place where many people go only at times when they want to remove the paper wrappings from candy bars and cough drops.

Concert Pitch: In the early history of music, pitch was

not standardized. It varied from country to country, and even from city to city. This made life very difficult for musicians who want to travel (and you thought *time zones* were a problem ...). Finally, after many attempts, a committee agreed in 1939 that pitch would be universally standardized and based upon A at 440 cycles per second. This made things much simpler for everyone, since now they all knew exactly what it was they were ignoring. Nowadays, A may be anywhere from about 425 to 450. Everyone agrees that concert pitch is a marvellous idea.

Concerto: A sort of musical boxing match between one musician (the soloist) and all the rest (the orchestra), with the conductor acting as referee, in which nobody wins — especially the audience.

Conductor: The person at the front of the orchestra or choir, facing away from the audience (usually out of embarrassment). The musical conductor should not be confused with the railway conductor, who probably has more training (nor indeed with the electrical conductor, which probably has more spark). In music, the conductor's primary function is to imitate a windmill, for the esthetic effect. The conductor's chief weapon is the baton, which everyone is pretending to watch carefully. If the performance goes well, the conductor takes all the credit; if badly, the performers get the blame.

Console: 1. (Noun) The area of a church organ where the player sits, containing the keyboards, pedals, stops, pistons and other gizmos, including spare eyeglasses, those funny shoes organists need, throat lozenges, old paper clips and wadded-up tissues.

A Conductor

2. (verb) The act of comforting organists after they perform a piece badly: "Don't worry, it was the postlude. Nobody heard the wrong notes because they all left before you started playing anyway." And so on.

Consonants: A subject of manic obsession among choirmasters. It's said that, by their use, one word may be distinguished from another. The origin of the myth is lost in the mists of Time and has never been successfully proven, since it's far beyond the capabilities of any singer.

Consumption: 1. A disease that's supposed to affect operatic sopranos in the role of Mimi (in Puccini's *La Boheme*). The audience is forced to accept that a 200-pound woman who sings for four hours is wasting away. Yeah, right.
2. The act of reverence that unites musicians and alcohol in large quantities.

Contralto: The second-highest vocal line sung by women (cf. *Counter-tenor*). Contraltos have a tendency to sing flat, and to sound like old molasses pudding. Derived from the Latin *altus*, which means "high." but which originally meant "overfed."

Copyist: A person hired by composers to transcribe pages of their illegible notation into other pages of the copyist's own notation, equally illegible.

Counterpoint: A musical device similar to needlepoint, although not designed to be hung on the wall or used on seatcovers. Said to be a musical conversation, it more often resembles an argument. A favourite device of

Counterpoint

many Baroque composers, all of whom are now dead — although a direct connection between these two facts has never been conclusively established. Although no longer in practice by modern composers, it's still taught in schools, as a form of punishment.

Counter-Tenor: The highest adult male voice currently available through legal and moral means. Sings roughly (and roughly sings) the same range as the contralto, although he can sing lower if pressed, and higher if pinched. Counter-tenors have a tendency to sing on pitch, but out of rhythm, and to sound like a cross between an oboe and a buzzsaw. Derived from the Latin *contra tenore*, which means "against tenors."

Critic: Most critics are themselves frustrated musicians who now bear a continual grudge against their more successful (?) colleagues. They are usually employed by newspapers, and their job consists of attending a performance and then producing an instant written pronouncement on its quality. Because these articles are continually written under the pressure of deadlines, late at night after the performance when the critic would much rather be asleep comfortably in bed, reviews more often than not reflect an attitude of crankiness and bad temper. On the rare occasions that the critic writes a favorable review, the performers are so overjoyed that they forgive all the nasty things said in the past — at least until the next time the critic pans their performance.

Crook: 1. A curved tube, part of a brass instrument, used for storing spit prior to its disposal onto the floor. 2. The type of person ideally suited for arts management.

Cross Relation: An angry relative.

Crwth: An ancient string instrument invented by the fiendish Welsh — and even harder to play than it is to pronounce or spell.

Cue: 1. An indication, especially from the conductor, that shows a musician when to enter.
2. A long, tapered wooden stick found in pool halls, and often used by an unemployed musician who has missed too many of the other kind of cues over the years.

Cycle: 1. In the music of Schubert, Schumann, Wolf and other German lieder lovers, a way of grouping songs together to tell a long and convoluted story.
2. A two-wheeled means of transportation useful for escaping from performances involving long, convoluted groups of songs.

D

Da Capo Aria: A particular type of aria with a built-in repeat, most often found in oratorio, opera and excess. Much favored by vain singers — there is no other kind — who are thus assured of at least one encore. Choirs have been known to stand up in the middle, to the confusion of the audience, who applaud half-heartedly.

D.C.: The abbreviation for Da Capo (Italian for "the head"), indicating a return to the start of a piece of music. Compare the indication Washington, D.C., so named because that's where the heads of the U.S. government reside.

Degree: A term for the steps of a scale — or for the piece of paper from the school at which you learned your scales in the first place.

Diction: That part of a singer's performance you can compliment when everything else is horrible. What most people really mean when they say diction is enunciation. Diction means the words chosen; enunciation means the clarity of their utterance. There's no sense complimenting singers on their diction, since the singers had nothing to do with the writing of the text. Trying to maintain this distinction, however, is a fruitless activity.

Diminished: In harmonic terminology, the term to

describe an interval that's been reduced by a small step. In financial terminology, the term to describe a musician's income after taxes.

Discord: 1. Not to be confused with datchord.
2. The emotional state that usually exists among a group of musicians, especially with regard to those in authority.

Dominant: What parents must be if they expect their small children to practise for music lessons.

Double Action: The pianist's term for a *ménage a trois*.

Double-Bass: *(Editor's note: The information contained in this entry is unavailable, due to an injunction against the author successfully obtained by the Society for the Prevention of Cruelty to Double-Basses and the People Who Play Them. The legal battles continue, but it is the Editor's hope that subsequent editions of this dictionary will be able to include this information in full.)*

Drums: A percussion instrument originally played on the battlefield to inspire the troops and frighten the enemy. Even in modern times drums retain their military connotations, being chiefly played by teenagers who wish to frighten their parents or by those wanting to do battle with the neighbors.

E

Early Music: In classical music, anything before about 1600. In rock music, anything before about noon.

Encore: A nasty method by which performers get back at the audience for its feigned appreciation in the form of applause. It consists of performing an extra piece "off the cuff" (which has been slavishly prepared for weeks). Audiences would be well advised not to applaud at all, so that everyone can get home that much sooner.

End-Plugged: The term for an organ pipe stopped at one end, which lowers its pitch by an octave. The term is sometimes also applied to organists themselves, because their cranky, distracted disposition is often the result of chronic constipation from sitting too long on organ benches.

English Horn: A woodwind instrument so named because it's neither English, nor a horn. Not to be confused with the French horn, which is German.

Ensemble: 1. (Noun) Any group of individual performers who are supposed to function as a unit.
2. (Adjective) the feeling of co-operation and togetherness that such groups lack.

Enunciation: What most people really mean when

The English Horn

they use to the term *diction* (see *Diction*).

Envelope: In electronic music, the term used to describe the growth and decay of a note or sound. In financial terms, the object containing a payment that determines the growth or decay of a musician's bank balance.

Exercise: A short activity — such as scales, arpeggios, small pieces — meant to improve a performer's technique by means of constant repetition. Also, any repetitive physical activity most usefully practised by overweight opera singers.

Exposition: In a fugue, the exposition is the musical equivalent of having wallpaper that matches the furniture.

Expression: 1. An indication in the score conveying information about tempo, dynamics, articulation or other means of shaping a musical phrase.
2. The pained look on the conductor's face when the performers ignore such indications.

F

Fancy: The term applied in the 16th century to certain light-hearted musical works and in the 20th to certain performers and the way they dress.

Fantasy: What most musicians have instead of a sex life.

False Relation: The kind of relative who is supportive of your musical career only if you're making money.

Fifth: A convenient quantity of alcohol to be consumed before, during or after a performance (see *Bar*).

Fitzwilliam Virginal Book: The famous book belonging to a notorious 16th-century rake, cad and womanizer named Thomas William Orlando Fitzwilliam, who was said to enjoy a challenge. It contains a list of the most desirable and innocent young ladies of Elizabethan London. Fitzwilliam died of old age and exhaustion, the day after his 23rd birthday.

Flageolet: A small end-blown flute used in early music and nowadays for performing Irish jigs and reels. Not to be confused with *flagellate*, the whipping we'd like to give some players after having to listen to too many jigs and reels.

Flat: An adjective used to describe a tone that's slightly below pitch. This term ought to be used cautiously, so as not to offend anyone, especially when applied to a woman.

Flats: Little marks that look like this: ♭ and which resemble small b's that have been deflated, or sat upon. They're similar to sharps, but different. Their function is to lower a note by a semi-tone (more or less). When gathered together at the beginning of a line, they form a key signature. This means that each corresponding note should be lowered by a semi-tone whenever it occurs, or whenever the performer remembers to do so. The double-flat lowers the note by two semi-tones, or one whole tone. This latter confusing distinction was invented solely to provide work for theorists and publishers.

Flute: A sophisticated peashooter with a range up to 500 yards and deadly accuracy in close quarters. Blown transversely to confuse the enemy, it can be dismantled into three small pieces, for easy concealment.

Form: 1. The shape of a composition.
2. The shape of the musician who plays the composition.
3. The piece of paper that must be completed in triplicate (known as ternary form) in order for the musician to get enough money from the arts council to play the composition.

French Horn: A brass instrument that resembles a snail, but sometimes moves more quickly. The complicated instrument of today is a direct descendant of the early horn used by hunters. It was originally long and straight, but got its present shape when trod upon by a

The Making of Flats

horse. The French horn is actually German, and should not be confused with the English horn, which is French.

Fugue: A type of Baroque composition similar to a crossword puzzle, but with fewer clues. The greatest fugue composer was J.S. Bach, who died before completing his seminal work, *The Art of Fugue*. Many musicians since have died trying to play it. (One misguided musicologist who thought that Fugue was actually an 18th-century portrait painter was unceremoniously drummed out of the profession, and has since made a fortune writing record-liner notes.)

G

Gapped: The term for a musical scale or melody with notes missing, or the smile of some performers with teeth missing. (Especially true of trumpet players in marching bands who don't watch where they're going.)

Glissando: The musical equivalent of stepping on a banana peel.

Grace Note: Every once in a while, the solo performer will attempt an interval, jumping from one note to another. In many instances, this is mere guesswork. If the wrong note is landed on, the performer may attempt to slide up or down to the correct one. The resulting confusion is politely called a *grace note*. A surprising term, since in many such instances, very little gracefulness is involved.

Grand: A term variously applied to a type of opera, a type of piano, a large musical staff or the thousand bucks you might earn for playing any one of them.

Grave: An Italian term meaning "slow" or "solemn." Appropriately enough, it's often found as a tempo indication in funeral music.

Gregorian Chant: A type of unison singing invented by monks as a mask for snoring.

Glissando

Groves, Sir George: Only one of many persons who may be turning over in their graves at this point.

H

Harmony: A sort of musical sociology. The study of the inter-relationship of individual notes and how they react in group encounters, such as tone-clusters and orgies. Theorists and others who study harmony have developed a highly intricate system of confusing terminology, to disguise the fact that they really don't know what's going on. The aspiring student of harmony should practise saying phrases such as "secondary sub-mediant appoggiatura six-four" or "first-inversion Neapolitan five-seven of five, sharp four plus eleven, going to a half-diminished seven of six" until they sound convincing. If unable to do this in a convincing manner, you may be in the wrong profession, or ought at least to consider becoming a critic, where even the most rudimentary knowledge of music isn't needed. It may, in fact, be a hindrance.

Harpsichord: A type of keyboard instrument, a precursor of the piano, and cursed at ever since. Sir Thomas Beecham described its sound as that of "two skeletons copulating on a corrugated tin roof."

Heel: The bottom end of the bow used by violinists, cellists and other players of bowed string instruments. By extension, then, the term is also often applied to the players themselves (see *Bent*, *Nut*).

Hemiola: A rhythmic device similar to a hernia.

Hidden Fifths: 1. In the strict rules of harmony and counterpoint, a stylistic error much deplored by pedantic professors.
2. A method by which many overstressed musicians, driven to drink (often by obscure and unreasonable rules of harmony and counterpoint imposed by their pedantic professors) help to calm their frazzled nerves.

I

Imitation: The sincerest form of counterpoint.

Inflection: 1. In plainchant, the term for those sections, especially at the beginning and end, more elaborate than the usual boring monotone bits.
2. A term for sharps, flats and other indications that raise or lower notes by a semi-tone or more. Not to be confused with *infection*, a virus prone to afflicting singers that often raises their temperature while lowering their vocal range by a semi-tone or more.

Instrument: That object by which many musicians make noise and earn their livelihoods. To a certain extent, a player can improve merely by replacing an old instrument by a better one (or, strangely with violins, a new instrument by an older one). This never happens as often as it should. Instruments, like their players, come in various shapes and sizes, and various degrees of unpleasantness.

Interval: 1. The distance, real or imagined, between two notes.
2. The British term for intermission — the break that gives performers a chance to go to the bathroom, and the audience a chance to sneak out early.
3. The waiting period between a performer's previous entry and the next. May vary from one bar to forever.

An Interval

Invention: 1. A short imitative work for two or three voices, much favored by J.S. Bach.

2. A facility other musicians might find useful, especially when preparing expense accounts or income-tax statements.

J

Jam: 1. A session at which jazz musicians improvise, usually late at night.
2. A sweet confection they spread on their toast the next morning.

Joint: 1. Especially in jazz or rock, musicians' slang for a bar, club or other venue where a performance takes place.
2. Also especially in jazz or rock, musicians' slang for the funny cigarette often consumed in such venues.

K

Kettledrums: Despite their name, these drums aren't very useful for making coffee or tea, since they're far too large and would take too long to boil the water. This is regrettable, since they aren't much use for anything else. Several composers in the past have used kettledrums to imitate sounds of battle and of rumbling thunder. Nowadays, they're used increasingly to imitate certain of the grosser bodily functions. Other than that, percussionists find them useful tables for chessboards.

Key: Certain musical terms defy easy definition. This is one of them.

Key Signature: As explained above (see *Flats*), a key signature is the attempt to organize what would otherwise be an unruly mob of accidentals into some sort of order at the beginning of each line of the staff. These sharps or flats (but rarely both) may number from none to seven, and their order and placement on the staff are rigidly controlled by music publishers, who are now too lazy to change their established typesetting. Several mnemonic phrases exist to help the musician remember the proper order of accidentals, the most useful being "Father Christmas gets diarrhea after eating biscuits" for the flats (or is it the sharps?) and — actually we can't remember the other one.

The Kettledrum

Klavierstück: A term used by German furniture movers trying to get a piano through a narrow doorway.

L

Laryngitis: The second-most effective and convincing way to silence a singer. The most effective way is death — though somewhat drastic, perhaps. It's only one of a large number of similar afflictions — such as the flu, colds, strep throat and *delirium tremens* — all of which have been known to affect singers at the least-opportune times. Such catastrophes are extremely prevalent among soloists, and have been known to lay waste to entire choirs at Christmas time.

Lay-Clerk: This term, used to describe certain types of singers in English cathedral and college choirs, is actually not as rude as it may appear.

Lust: 1. The German word for "light," as in the prisoners' chorus *O Welche Lust*, from Beethoven's opera *Fidelio*.
2. The sort of feeling likely to interfere with a musician's practice time, not to mention good judgment (see *Passion, Rhapsody*).

Lute: A string instrument of the Medieval and Renaissance periods, resembling a bloated guitar. It was frequently used to provide background music at mealtimes. It can have as many as 16 sets of strings (most of them in pairs), which are referred to as "courses." (With 16 courses at mealtime, no wonder it was bloated.) It gets its name from the Arabic *el oude*, the meaning of which has, until recently, eluded musicologists — who are the only ones who would care, anyway. It's now known that the name comes from the practice of using this instrument to accompany lewd songs.

M

Madrigal: A type of part-song, popular in the Renaissance, for unaccompanied voices. Often involves one of the earliest examples of censorship in music: Some of the refrains were so lewd and suggestive that they had to be replaced by repetitions of "fa-la-la." (Pedantic musicologists — there is no other kind — may at this point mention that the proper term for such a madrigal is "ballett." Humor them and they may go away.)

Mediation: 1. In plainchant, a form of inflection at the end of the first section of a psalm (see *Inflection*, not to be confused with *infection*).
2. A form of legal negotiation sometimes resorted to among musicians when contract talks break down. Not to be confused with *medication*, the drugs the musicians might have to take in order to survive the mediation process.

Messiah: An oratorio by Handel, attempted every Christmas by some choir that thinks it's good enough, and in collaboration with instrumentalists, who need the money. It's the musical equivalent of death and taxes: inescapable and excruciating.

Mezzo-Soprano: A sort of half-hearted (sometimes half-witted) soprano. Marginally more intelligent, due to the reduced effect of high notes, which addle the brain.

Handel's 'Messiah'

Mixture: 1. For organs, the blending of certain pipes to obtain a more pleasing sound.
2. For organists, the blending of certain alcoholic ingredients to obtain a more pleasing beverage, or to drown out the sound of certain organ pipes.

Modern Music: The name given in polite company to the present mess we're in. It's important to remember that musical styles are rarely popular when they're new and current, and rarely unpopular when they're old and established. The music of Beethoven, for example, was considered far too "modern" when he wrote it. But of course nowadays the music of Beethoven is considered wonderful and great. It's a frightening prospect to consider that the same may be said of today's music, a hundred years from now.

Modes: Groups into which notes were organized before the invention of scales, the introduction of which caused them to become out-moded.

Modulation: A means of getting from one key to another, similar to changing lanes on the highway, and just as hazardous if done recklessly. Unsuccessful modulations may lead to atonality — a sort of 12-car pileup.

Music: 1. Any combination of sounds and words, akin to noise and cacophony, produced (intentionally or by accident) by musicians (also, though rarely, by singers).
2. The printed form of obscure hieroglyphics, squiggles, scrawls and blots that purport to tell the musician how to produce the desired noise. It may be (a) illegible, (b) boring, (c) too difficult, or (d) any combination thereof. The production of music follows three stages.

It is:
1. set down by the composer
2. Interpreted (incorrectly) by the conductor and
3. Ignored by the performers and audience.

Music Lesson: A form of cruel and unusual punishment inflicted on young children by their parents, and on teachers by their shrinking bank balances. In such instances, it's a debatable point which is more unbalanced — the bank account or the music teacher.

Music Stand: An intricate device for propping up music, except at crucial times — such as during the performance. It has a tendency to fall over, often of its own accord. It comes in two sizes — too high or too low — and is always broken.

Musica Ficta: Ancient rules for the interpretation of Early Music. A sort of musical *Everyday Etiquette*. In Medieval times, the principles of *ficta* were understood by everybody, so they were never written down. Nowadays, nobody can write them down, because nobody understands them at all.

Musicians: Individuals bent upon producing sound or noise by means of scraping, hitting, beating or blowing into an object made of wood, brass or catgut. In a performance, each may be seen wearing an ill-fitting tuxedo or black dress. (In most cases, the men wear tuxedos and the women wear dresses.) Orchestral musicians are allowed to sit, for which they get paid extra. Choral musicians rarely get paid at all, and they must stand throughout the performance, unless they faint. Most musicians can count to at least four, and

The Musicians' Union

some to five. Not to be confused with *singers*.

Musicians' Union: A powerful branch of the Mafia that controls the exorbitant amounts of money paid to musicians, and also the number of coffee breaks permitted per hour (at least one, and usually three, with pay). Singers, not being musicians, aren't required to be members. All others must join, the penalty being blacklisting, or preferably death.

Mute: A device for muffling the sound of certain instruments — notably the trumpet, trombone and violin — reducing their tone from excruciating to merely annoying. Unfortunately, efforts to design mutes for certain other instruments — the bagpipes and accordion spring immediately to mind — have been less successful.

N

Node: 1. The point of rest between two portions of a vibrating string.

2. A sign of strain that sometimes afflicts singers who have injured their vocal cords.

3. In less severe cases, that portion of a singer's facial anatomy that gets all stuffy during a bad cold or nasal infection. (Among singers, this is known as having "a code in de node.")

Noise: A more accurate term for sound.

None: 1. In Gregorian tradition, one of several liturgical services held throughout the day, this one "at the ninth hour" — that is, three o'clock in the morning.

2. The number of listeners likely to show up at any such service held at three o'clock in the morning.

Notes: Little black dots with stems and flags that are the peculiar language of music. The "whole" note is divided into "halves," "quarters" and so on. These divisions are usually referred to as "long," "short" and "really short." Widely held to be understood by musicians (and sometimes by singers), they are, in fact, a bafflement to all — but everyone is too proud to admit it.

Nut: The narrow ridge across the neck of a string instrument such as the violin, situated near the pegbox. By extension, then, the term has come to be applied to any person who plays such an instrument (see *Bent*, *Heel*).

O

Oboe: An ill wind that nobody blows good.

Octave: A distance of approximately eight notes (12 if it includes all semi-tones, as many as 27 if sung by a tenor).

Opera: A performance involving singers with orchestra (complete with unrealistic scenery and silly costumes), which tells a story so complex that nobody in the audience understands what's going on, although all speak about it as if they did. Consists mainly of fat people bellowing in a foreign language.

Opera Buffa: Not, as you might expect, opera in the nude. Not yet, anyway.

Orchestra: The result of musicians' having discovered that there's safety in numbers. So much so that the orchestra often outnumbers its audience. Can be distinguished from a mob only by the fact that a mob chooses weapons such as placards and stones, while an orchestra chooses weapons such as violins and trumpets. Also, mobs rarely wear black.

Orchestra Pit: 1. A deep hole, in the front of and below the stage, where the orchestra performs and into which things (including persons) have a tendency to fall.
2. (Doubtful) That part of an orchestra which is left

The Orchestra Pit

Ornamentation

over when one has digested all of the rest, and which ought to be spat into the garbage (cf. cherries, peaches, avocados, etc.) or planted. Science has, as yet, been unable to cultivate an orchestra by this method, although some of its failures are no worse than many orchestras already in existence.

Organ: A mythical instrument, part man and part beast, known to inhabit churches — especially ones that are cold, damp, drafty and impoverished. In constant need of repairs and impossible to tune, it has a very large range: The highest notes attract bats, and the lowest loosen the floorboards. Everything in between sounds like a cross between thunderous cisterns and cold porridge. Most often used to accompany choirs, and to provide background noise for the church service. It can also be an effective means of suppressing sermons.

Organist: The person hired by a church to play the organ and to provide music for services, weddings, funerals and other joyous occasions. Not to be confused with the *organ student*, who actually *does* the playing.

Organ Student: A species of sub-organist, or a subspecies of organist.

Ornamentation: 1. The practice of adding extra notes to a melody in order to improve it, or to disguise one's inability to perform it properly.
2. The only reason some persons are allowed to remain in a musical organization.

P

Passion: 1. One of any number of long-winded oratorios by Bach or others, telling the death and resurrection of Christ. Usually told in the version according to one of the four Gospels. (*The Passion According to Reuters' Jerusalem Correspondent* has not received the attention it deserves.) The performance is ideally suited to the Easter season, since at the end the audience has the feeling of having eaten too many Easter eggs, and the performers feel as if they've laid one.
2. The sort of feeling that's apt to interfere with a musician's practice time, not to mention meals (see *Lust, Rhapsody*).

Pedal-Point: Not to be confused with counterpoint or needlepoint. A compositional device, used especially in pieces for the organ (which badly need it), by which the listener is forewarned that the end is near (of the music, that is). It consists of a long-held note in the bass, sometimes the result of the organist's foot having gone to sleep.

Pedals: A special keyboard on the organ, operated by the player's feet, used for the lowest bass notes. Unlike bicycles and tricycles, which also have pedals, there's little to be gained — and much to be lost — by pedalling the organ as fast as you can.

Pencil: This small object is what distinguishes the professional musician from the mere amateur. No self-respecting musician should be without one, and union imposes heavy fines on anyone unable to produce one, like a union card, on demand. For this reason, pencils should be zealously guarded, as they have a habit of disappearing. (They often reappear in the possession of a nearby musician, under circumstances suspiciously resembling theft.) Keeping the pencil sharp is another problem altogether — one of the few times that sharpness can be an asset. Courses in this art have recently been introduced at some of the more progressive music schools.

Performance: The main reason for the getting-together of any number of musicians, usually to perform a piece of music (ideally, all at the same time). It's the best excuse for a large, drunken party — although any excuse will do.

Piano: A cumbersome piece of furniture found in many homes, where playing it ensures the early departure of unwanted guests.

Piano Tuner: A person employed to come into the home, rearrange the furniture and annoy the cat. The tuner's chief purpose is to ascertain the breaking-point of the piano strings.

Pitch: 1. The relative highness or lowness of a musical note, and the ability to control the same. For an interesting discussion of the curious overlap of terminology between music and baseball, the inquiring reader is referred to the seminal treatise on the subject: *Das kuriosen überlappisch Terminologichen zwishen*

Pitch

Musik und Baseball und warum es Samstag immer regnet (Munchen: Ashenbecker Verlag) 1897, rev. 1926. 2. Another name for tar — which, along with a bag of feathers, is an essential ingredient for punishing those performers (especially singers) unable to control the relative highness or lowness of a note.

Podium: A raised platform given to conductors to make them feel more important than they really are. From the podium, the conductor can look over the orchestra and overlook its mistakes.

Polytonality: A pathological disease most likely to affect composers of modern music. A mild form of *atonality*. Since one of its characteristics is the evidence of a sense of confusion, it's often hard to detect — that being the usual state of many musicians and composers. Nevertheless, this particular confusion tends to manifest itself in a desire to be "all things to all men," at least as regards key and key signature.

Prima Donna: The most important female role in an opera. This is, of course, largely a matter of opinion. By extension, the term has come to be applied to any singer who merely behaves as if hers is the most important role — that's to say, everyone. Derived from an Italian phrase that may be roughly translated as "pain in the neck," although some have a lower opinion.

Prodigy: A person who shows tremendous musical talent at a very early age. Mozart, one of music's greatest prodigies, set the example later followed by others by dying at age 36. Those wishing to be considered prodigy material would be well advised to die young, before

A Prodigy

it becomes apparent that they aren't going to get any better, and while the reduced union rates for children still apply.

Program Notes: Short essays, filled with useless and unverified (i.e. untrue) information about composers and their music, provided as a supplement to the performance. They are intended to furnish insight into the music, on the fanciful theory that a well-informed audience is an appreciative audience. In fact, it's probably better to keep audiences in the dark — figuratively speaking. They're already literally in the dark, which makes it impossible to read the program notes anyway. At any rate, all of this is a moot point, since the program will be changed at the last minute, and it will bear no relation to what's written in the notes.

Q

Quartet: 1. Formerly, all that remained of the Moscow Philharmonic Orchestra after its North American tour. Now, in these times of cutbacks, all that remains of just about *any* orchestra after the salary budget is set. 2. The number of players in most orchestras who are worth hanging on to anyway.

Quasi: An Italian term for "almost," meaning "in the style of" (as in Beethoven's *Moonlight Sonata*, described as *quasi una fantasia* — as if it were a fantasia). Not to be confused with *queasy*, the sort of feeling a nervous performer might get before having to play Beethoven's *Moonlight Sonata*.

Quaver: What many performers do while performing.

R

Racket: A Renaissance wind instrument that resembles a coffee can with a double reed sticking out the top. Possibly so named because it makes a lot of noise.

Radical Bass: 1. Same as *fundamental bass* — the bass line (often imaginary) derived from having each chord in its root position.
2. The type of singer who hung around Berkeley in the '60s.

Rank: 1. In church organs, the term for a particular grouping of pipes.
2. Also in church organs, the term for the awful sound those pipes sometimes make.

Rant: 1. An old English dance of the 17th century.
2. The kind of screaming fit or tantrum temperamental musicians are sometimes prone to, often after having to play (or worse, dance) too many of the above.

Rattle: 1. A noisemaking toy given to amuse a fussy baby.
2. A small instrument used by percussion players — many of whom are just fussy babies anyway.

Recital: A performance by a soloist or small group of musicians, more intimate and often shorter than a concert — but nevertheless still not short enough to avoid being tiresome. Not to be confused with *rectal*, a kind of intimate and intrusive medical examination often less painful to endure than some recitals.

Recitative: Gossip set to music. A device in opera and oratorio for getting large chunks of narration over with quickly. Unfortunately, this leaves more time to be spent on long-winded arias.

Reeds: A family of instruments that includes the clarinet, oboe, bassoon and kazoo. The name derives from the material that vibrates to produce the sound. Many reeds would be better off left in the swamp.

Refrain: 1. That part of a song that keeps being repeated, ad nauseam.
2. What most performers should do.

Rehearsal: Ideally, a meeting of musicians (and singers) for the purpose of becoming familiar with the music. In fact, a social occasion where little if any work is done. Most useful for the repetition of mistakes.

Rehearsal Letter: 1. A letter of the alphabet written into the score and the individual parts of a piece of music. The placement of the letter corresponds to the number of the bar, and is intended as a reference point to facilitate rehearsal. That's the theory, anyway. Unfortunately, the letter often appears at a different place in each part, leading to mass confusion.
2. A note from your mother explaining why you were late or missed last week's rehearsal.

Relative: 1. The term used to describe a major and

A Rest

minor key that share the same key signature.

2. The person you might count on to attend your performance when no one else bothers to come — or at least to buy a ticket, if only out of a sense of family obligation.

Repertoire: The large number of standard pieces of music with which an orchestral musician must claim to be familiar in order to secure a position in a major orchestra. Also, the pieces that a singer is likely to forget at any given time. The American Civil War hero General Ulysses S. Grant made the definitive comment on repertoire when he remarked: "I only know two tunes. One of them is *Yankee Doodle*. The other one isn't."

Resolution: 1. In harmony, the successful movement from a discordant note to a more harmonious one.

2. In contract negotiations, pretty much the same situation (see *Mediation*).

Resonance: A quality of tone that most musicians strive for, and that singers have in their head voice instead of brains (see *Brain*).

Rest: A short period of relative silence in an individual part, useful for turning pages, breathing, cleaning out spit-valves, coughing and so forth. Rarely found in Baroque music, union regulations now exist to govern the number of rests required in each piece of music (usually one per bar, or 15 minutes of every hour).

Rhapsody: A heightened emotional state likely to interfere with a musician's practice time, not to mention sleep (see *Lust, Passion*).

Rhythm: 1. A faculty in great demand and, unfortunately, in very short supply among those involved in music. 2. An unreliable method for curtailing the population of musicians.

Round: 1. A short, simple, repetitive piece of music similar to a canon, but less likely to misfire.
2. The shape eventually achieved by many musicians, especially opera singers.

Rubato: The term used to describe the erratic behavior of a performer in the throes of anguish brought on by the mating season. Especially prevalent in tenors.

Runs: An ailment particularly prevalent among singers of Baroque music, especially that of Bach and Handel. Can often be remedied by proper diet.

S

Scale: 1. A stepwise collection of notes often played as a warmup exercise.
2. The rate of pay determined by the union and given to musicians who diligently practise their warmup exercises.

Score: An amalgamation of all the individual parts, transposed into the key of C, so that no one else can understand it. This is what conductors conduct from, and they are supposed to have studied it carefully. Most conductors, however, don't know the score.

Scoring: 1. The art of assigning parts to various instruments or singers.
2. The finer art of assigning private parts to various instruments or singers (see *Action, Double Action*).

Serial Music: Not to be confused with early morning, or cereal music. The result of a method of composition using all 12 notes of the scale in some established order. Despite this, the result is often chaos.

Sharp: 1. Adjective used to describe a tone that's slightly above pitch (cf. *Flat.* Not so easily misconstrued.)
2. Adjective used to describe a nattily attired colleague.

Sharps: Little marks that look like this: # and that

would be useful for playing Xs and Os during the more boring moments of a performance if they weren't so small. They're similar to flats, but different. Their function is to raise a note by a semi-tone (more or less). They may also be gathered to form key signatures. For an explanation of the double-sharp, read the entry for *Flats* and figure it out for yourself. There may be a short quiz at the end of this book.

Singer: A special type of musician, notable for the inability to count at all. Unlike other musicians, who must rely on an instrument to produce sound, singers use only what they call "the vocal apparatus" (and what ordinary people would call "the voice"). There are certain inherent advantages and disadvantages: On the one hand, singers wishing to improve their technique can't simply buy better instruments — but then some of the carrying cases are so much more attractive.

Snob, Musical: Someone who pretends to know more about music than we pretend to.

Solo: A device that makes it easier to place the blame for mistakes entirely on one individual. The other device that facilitates this is called the *Conductor*.

Soloists: Individuals whose egos are larger than both their brains and their ability combined, and equalled in some cases only by their greed. Soloists can be of two types, either (a) good or (b) bad. The latter are more common. In fact, the former exist only in theoretical treatises, and have never been known to exist in real life. Certainly never in real performances.

Sonata Form: The development of Sonata Form (also called Sonata Allegro Form or First Movement Form) is one of the most fascinating topics in the study of music, since it combines elements of history, theory, analysis and composition. It also involves all of the major composers of Western music. We wish we had more time to talk about it.

Soprano: The highest vocal line, sung by women (but cf. *Treble*). Sopranos have a tendency to sing sharp, and to sound like fingernails scraped on chalkboard. Not to be confused with *soaprano*, a woman who sprayed her throat from the wrong bottle on the bathroom counter. Derived from the Latin *superius*, which means "highest." This has given many sopranos a superiority complex, exceedingly unfounded. Sopranos tend to be the most feeble-minded of all the singing voices. This may be explained by the fact that notes of higher frequency travel directly to the brain (but see *Brain*) and cause rapid decay.

Sound: 1. A polite term for noise.
2. A type of mental attitude rarely obtained by musicians, even more rarely by conductors and never by singers.

Species: 1. In Early Music, a term for designating various classes of counterpoint.
2. A term for designating various classes of musicians. (Usually the human species — but with some of them, you can't always tell.)

Stop: 1. A device on the organ, which changes the sound of a note from disagreeable to annoying.

A Soaprano

2. What organists should do to improve their playing (see *Refrain*).

Stringendo: Also *string-endo*. The term applied to a demised violin.

Strings: 1. A family of instruments that includes the violin, viola, cello, double-bass and yo-yo. The strings used in producing the sound were originally manufactured out of catgut. This may be responsible for their ear-piercing tone, which continues even in these days of synthetic string material. Ancient violin makers believed that the best strings were made from female cats in heat, as evidenced by the violin's characteristic screech. 2. What many musicians need to pull in order to land a decent job — or even *any* job.

T

Te Deum: A particular work set by various composers for use during a church service. Not to be confused with *tedium*, the feeling you often get from listening to such works.

Temperament: 1. A set of guidelines for tuning instruments, chiefly keyboards.
2. The state of mind that quickly deteriorates when such guidelines are applied incompetently.

Tempo: The speed at which music travels. Said to be controlled by the conductor, but in reality by the players. It may vary from piece to piece, and certainly from player to player. It's always faster in performance than it has been in rehearsal, usually by a factor of two.

Tenor: A high-pitched male voice, akin to screaming. Extremely rare, so usually sung by frustrated baritones whose reach exceeds their grasp. Tenors have a tendency to sing off-pitch, out of time, out of control and to sound like a strangulating cat. Derived from the Latin *tenor*, which means "to hold" (cf. *tenacious, tenuous, tentative*).

Tie: 1. A small, curved mark that joins together two notes.
2. A small black piece of cloth that joins together the front of a musician's shirt collar.

Tone: 1. That aspect of a singer's performance you can compliment when you can't understand the words (see *Diction*).

2. The interval of the distance between two adjacent notes. Can be either a whole tone or a semi-tone. Occasional use of quarter-tones has not been successful, since musicians have difficulty dealing with fractions smaller than halves.

Tone Cluster: A kind of chordal orgy, a smorgasbord of musical notes. First discovered by a very well-endowed lady pianist, while leaning forward to turn a page.

Tonic: A medicinal libation usefully consumed before a performance — and even more usefully so afterward.

Transposition: 1. The act of moving the relative pitch of a piece of music that's too low for the basses up to a point where it's too high for the sopranos.

2. A method of ensuring that no musician will be able to read a part belonging to another musician, by writing each part in a different key. Through some miracle not as yet understood by theorists, the parts usually sound right together. The conductor retaliates by transposing everything into the key of C (see *Score*) to confuse the musicians, and because that's the only key that most conductors can read, even a little bit. The main purpose of transposition is to provide work for copyists.

Treble: A small boy used especially in Anglican church choirs to sing the highest vocal line (under other circumstances sung by a soprano). Those who favor this type of choral sound maintain that all the effort it takes to properly train small boys is worthwhile, because the end result is so pleasing — and because they are usually the boys' mothers. In addition to the usual skills of sight-reading and interpretation, boys must be taught forms of self-discipline such as bladder control. Often, the former is easer than the latter. Not to be confused with *trouble*, although the two generally amount to the same thing.

Triangle: 1. A small high-pitched instrument used by percussionists chiefly to annoy the rest of the orchestra. 2. A romantic configuration not advised for musicians wishing to avoid heartache, embarrassment, financial ruin or legal proceedings (see *Double Action*).

Trill: The musical equivalent of an epileptic seizure.

Trio Sonata: An instrumental piece popular in the Baroque, so called because it has parts for four players. This is the same sort of logic that accounts for the theorist's calling the combined intervals of an octave and a third a 10th ($8+3=10$ — what could be more sensible than that?). The inherent fallibility of this reasoning has not seemed to dismay musicians over the centuries, so we shouldn't let it trouble us now. Strangely enough, musicians' inability to count properly disappears whenever they're calculating their wages.

Trombone: A slide whistle with delusions of grandeur.

Tuxedo: A type of ill-fitting black suit worn by male musicians during a performance. It's purchased at a local Salvation Army store (or — preferably — borrowed from another musician) and must be at least 10 years old. It's either too large or too small, too baggy or too tight. Footwear accompanying the tuxedo is very occasionally a pair of black dress shoes (rarely polished), but more often sneakers, brown loafers, or sandals. The addition of a questionable white shirt and a bowtie (either black or rainbow-colored) completes the outfit. The ownership of a tuxedo is mandatory for male musicians — much like a fez for Shriners. The female equivalent of the tuxedo is any dress, knee-length or longer, that's vaguely black (i.e. black, grey, brown, blue, purple, chartreuse, etc.).

U

Unessential Notes: A relative term — one that never applies to your own notes, but only to those of other performers (see *Wrong Notes*).

Unison: The sound of two or more musicians performing the same note or part at exactly the same time. (Note: Like the speed of light, absolute zero and various other philosophical and scientific Holy Grails, this is a theoretical concept only. It's never actually been achieved in a real performance.)

V

Valve: A means of changing the direction of the flow of air (and spit) in the tube of a brass instrument. Similar to a highway detour, but less likely to require a map.

Variation: The sort of tune written by composers who can never make up their minds.

Verismo: A style of writing opera that attempts to make the characters and situations more lifelike and realistic. Since the terms "opera" and "realism" are mutually exclusive, *verismo* — like Santa Claus and the Tooth Fairy — can never really exist at all.

Vibraphone: A xylophone with stage fright.

Vibrato: A technique used by certain instruments, said to add warmth and body to the tone, and used by singers to hide the fact that they're on the wrong pitch.

Viol: One of a family of bowed string instruments, popular in the Renaissance, that became the forerunners of the modern violin family. Opinion is divided on which of the two instruments, ancient or modern, is more vile than the other.

Viola: A relative of the violin, a sort of poor cousin.

Vibrato

Violin: The squeakiest member of the string family. It tends to get its way in an orchestra because violins outnumber the other instruments.

Virginal: A keyboard instrument similar to the harpsichord, so called because of the sorts of ladies who were supposed to have played it in the 16th century — and if you believe that, you'll believe anything.

Voluntary: The name given to a piece for organ often played at the end of a church service. The terminology is puzzling and ironic, since under such circumstances one's decision to endure the assault is far from voluntary.

Wind: The essential ingredient needed to produce sound from many instruments. It's possessed in large quantities by conductors, who have very little need for it, except for bellowing at the players.

Woodwinds: A family of instruments so called because its members are made of wood. This includes the flute (which is made of silver), the saxophone (made of brass) and the bassoon (often made of plastic). The woodwind family includes all the members of the reed family, as well as others, such as the flute, that would otherwise feel left out. Like most families, the members often quarrel.

Wrong Notes: A relative term (see *Unessential Notes*), applying only to those examples performed by someone else. Wrong notes you perform yourself are always referred to as "ornaments."

Woodwind

X

Xylophone: An instrument of the percussion family. Its chief claim to fame is that its name begins with an "x" — the only instrument so honored (well, except for the xylomarimba, but that's pretty much the same thing). Consequently, it's extremely useful for compilers of music dictionaries.

Y

Yawn: The act of opening the mouth wide to take in breath. Usually the result of boredom or lack of sleep, it's generally considered bad form to yawn during a concert — especially if you're one of the performers.

Z

Z: The sound made by members of the audience during a performance (especially of opera). Usually found in the plural, thus: ZZZZZZ. Often accompanied by a snore.

About the Author

David Barber is a journalist and musician and the author of seven other books of musical history and humor. Formerly entertainment editor of the *Kingston Whig-Standard* and editor of *Broadcast Week* magazine at the *Toronto Globe and Mail*, he is now a freelance journalist in Toronto. As a composer, his works include two symphonies, a jazz mass based on the music of Dave Brubeck, a *Requiem*, several short choral and chamber works and various vocal-jazz arrangements. An avid kayaker and reader of detective mysteries, he also enjoys singing with his vocal-jazz group, Barber & the Sevilles.

About the Cartoonist

Dave Donald can't remember when he didn't scrawl his little marks on most surfaces, so it doesn't come as much of a surprise that he now makes a living doing just that. He is currently balancing a steady job as an art director at a Toronto magazine with his more abstruse artistic pursuits. This book represents his first of seven illustrative collaborations with David Barber.

A Musician's Dictionary

© David W. Barber, 1983, 1990, 1997
© Dave Donald (cartoons), 1983, 1985, 1988, 1990

All Rights Reserved

Published in Canada by

SOUND AND VISION
359 Riverdale Avenue
Toronto, Canada M4J 1A4

First printing, August 1983
Revised edition, August 1997
19 21 23 25 27 - printings - 26 24 22 20 18

Canadian Cataloguing in Publication Data

Barber, David W. (David William), 1958-
A musician's dictionary

ISBN 0-920151-21-3

1. Music - Humor. I. Donald, David C. II. Title
ML65.B234 1997   780' .207   C97-931527-1

Typeset in Century Expanded

Printed and bound in Canada

Other Sound And Vision books by David W. Barber,
with cartoons by Dave Donald:

Bach, Beethoven and the Boys
Music History as It Ought to Be Taught
preface by Anthony Burgess
ISBN 0-920151-10-8

When the Fat Lady Sings
Opera History as It Ought to Be Taught
preface by Maureen Forrester
foreword by Anna Russell
ISBN 0-920151-34-5

If It Ain't Baroque
More Music History as It Ought to Be Taught
ISBN 0-920151-15-9

Getting a Handel on Messiah
preface by Trevor Pinnock
ISBN 0-920151-17-5

Tenors, Tantrums and Trills
An Opera Dictionary from Aida to Zzzz
ISBN 0-920151-19-1

Tutus, Tights and Tiptoes
Ballet History as It Ought to Be Taught
preface by Karen Kain
ISBN 0-920151-30-2

by David W. Barber (Editor):

Better Than It Sounds
A Dictionary of Humorous Musical Quotations
ISBN 0-920151-22-1

Other musical humor books from Sound And Vision:

The Thing I've Played With The Most
Prof. Anthon E. Darling Discusses His Favourite Instrument
by David E. Walden, cartoons Mike Duncan
ISBN 0-920151-35-3

1812 And All That
A Concise History of Music from 30.000 BC to the Millennium
by Lawrence Leonard, cartoons Emma Bebbington
ISBN 0-920151-33-7

Opera Antics & Anecdotes
by Stephen Tanner, cartoons Umberto Tàccola
foreword David W. Barber
ISBN 0-920151-32-9

How To Listen To Modern Music
Without Earplugs
by David E. Walden, cartoons Mike Duncan
foreword Bramwell Tovey
ISBN 0-920151-31-0

The Composers
A Hystery of Music
by Kevin Reeves, preface Daniel Taylor
ISBN 0-920151-29-9

A Working Musician's Joke Book
by Daniel G. Theaker, cartoons Mike Freen
preface David W. Barber
ISBN 0-920151-23-X

How To Stay Awake
During Anybody's Second Movement
by David E. Walden, cartoons Mike Duncan
preface Charlie Farquharson
ISBN 0-920151-20-5

Love Lives of the Great Composers
From Gesualdo to Wagner
by Basil Howitt
ISBN 0-920151-18-3

I Wanna Be Sedated
Pop Music in the Seventies
by Phil Dellio & Scott Woods, cartoons Dave Prothero
preface Chuck Eddy
ISBN 0-920151-16-7

THE THING I'VE PLAYED WITH THE MOST

Professor Anthon E. Darling
Discusses His Favourite Instrument

DAVID E. WALDEN

CARTOONS BY
MIKE DUNCAN

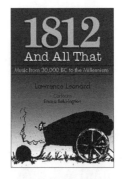

1812

And All That

Music from 30,000 BC to the Millennium

Lawrence Leonard

Cartoons by
Emma Bebbington

How to Listen to Modern Music

Without Earplugs

DAVID E. WALDEN

CARTOONS BY
MIKE DUNCAN

FOREWORD BY BRAMWELL TOVEY

The **COMPOSERS**
A Hystery of Music

KEVIN REEVES

PREFACE BY
DANIEL TAYLOR

A Working Musician's

Joke Book

Daniel G. Theaker

David W. Barber   Mike Finch

THE AVERAGE MUSIC LOVER'S GUIDE TO CONCERTGOING

HOW TO STAY AWAKE

DURING ANYBODY'S SECOND MOVEMENT

DAVID E. WALDEN

ILLUSTRATIONS
MIKE DUNCAN

PREFACE
CHARLIE FARQUHARSON

Love Lives
of the
Great Composers

Basil Howitt

I WANNA BE SEDATED

POP MUSIC IN THE SEVENTIES

by
PHIL DELLIO & SCOTT WOODS

ILLUSTRATIONS
DAVE PROTHERO

NOTE FROM THE PUBLISHER

Sound And Vision books may be purchased for educational or promotional use or for special sales. If you have any comments on this book or any other book we publish or if you would like a catalogue, please write to us at:
Sound And Vision, 359 Riverdale Avenue,
Toronto, Canada M4J 1A4.
Or visit our web site at: www.soundandvision.com.
We would really like to hear from you.

We are always looking for original books to publish. If you have an idea or manuscript that is in the genre of musical humour including educational themes, please contact us at our address. Thank you for purchasing or borrowing this book.

Geoffrey Savage
Publisher